Workbook

For

Lysa TerKeurst's

Forgiving What You Can't Forget

Smart Reads

Note to readers:
This is an unofficial workbook for Lysa
TerKeurst's "Forgiving What You Can't
Forget" designed to enrich your reading
experience. The original book can be
purchased on Amazon.

Download Your Free Gift

As a way to say "Thank You" for being a fan of our series,
I've included a free gift for you:

Brain Health: How to Nurture and Nourish Your Brain For
Top Performance

Go to www.smart-reads.com to get your
FREE book.

The Smart Reads Team

Table of Contents

Overview of *Forgiving What You Can't Forget: Discover How to Move On, Make Peace with Painful Memories, and Create a Life That's Beautiful Again*

"Forgiving What You Can't Forget" by Lysa TerKeurst is a transformative book that delves into the profound and challenging journey of forgiveness. Drawing from her personal experiences, she compassionately explores the depths of pain, betrayal, and heartache that can often make forgiveness seem impossible.

Through her authentic storytelling and relatable insights, she guides readers on a path toward healing and freedom. She offers practical strategies and actionable steps to help readers navigate through the complex emotions associated with forgiveness. From acknowledging and processing hurt to setting healthy boundaries, she provides invaluable tools to aid in the forgiveness process.

One of the book's key strengths lies in its emphasis on self-compassion and self-care. She explains the difficulty of forgiveness and the need for individuals to prioritize their own well-being. She encourages readers to extend grace to themselves, offering gentle reminders that healing takes time and patience.

Furthermore, "Forgiving What You Can't Forget" addresses the spiritual aspect of forgiveness, highlighting the transformative power it holds for both the forgiver and the forgiven. She explores the profound connection between forgiveness and faith, providing readers with biblical wisdom and heartfelt prayers to guide them on their journey.

Ultimately, this book offers a roadmap for those who long to break free from the chains of unforgiveness and discover the profound peace and liberation that forgiveness brings. With its blend of vulnerability, empathy, and practical guidance, "Forgiving What You Can't Forget" is a compelling resource for anyone seeking to heal their hearts, restore relationships, and find true emotional freedom.

Chapter 1 – Forgiveness, the Double-Edged Word

During the early days of her marriage devastation, Lysa desired to escape the emotional pain by being anesthetized like during surgery. The continuous shocks, heartbreak, and damage affected every aspect of her life, causing struggles with her children, declining health, financial difficulties, and unexpected legal issues. Sleep became her only escape, as she clung to the hope that the next day would bring improvement. However, time passed, and she gradually transformed into someone unrecognizable, plagued by anxiety, panic attacks, and overwhelming pain. Her once optimistic outlook turned dark, relationships became burdensome, and happiness felt forced. As the weight of her experiences settled in, she felt like the soldiers of unforgiveness were waging war against her. These soldiers were namely cynicism; assuming all people are motivated by self-interest and hence if she'd hoped for less, she will not get hurt, bitterness; holding onto all evidence of her pain so that she can make them feel guilty continuously, resentment; believing that the only way to ease the pain is if her wrongdoers felt equally hurt, delay; in letting go of the pain which stopped her from picking herself up again and trust issues; believing everyone is out to hurt her and that no one is truly honest. Forgiveness, a concept she initially embraced, became challenging in the face of her suffering.

She reflected on how it seemed strange for her to pen the words of the book, having struggled with forgiveness herself. Forgiveness could feel offensive and impossible, aggravating the sense of injustice. She shared a story from her college days when she held onto a minor conflict, staying in the parking lot to prove a point, while her friends enjoyed a beach outing. She realized that her refusal to let go only affected her, leaving her hungry, lonely, and defeated. The soldiers of unforgiveness celebrated their victory that day, leading her to isolation, broken relationships, and a darkened outlook. She emphasized the power of forgiveness as a weapon and the importance of making choices to move forward. With an assurance of grace and fueled by God's truth, the book aimed to guide softening fearful hearts and finding healing.

Forgiveness can be a double-edged sword. It is hard to give but easy to get, and when the Lord gives it to us freely, and we do not do the same, it creates a weight in our hearts, the weight of forgiveness. To forgive is not just a difficult choice you make on your own; it is made possible by cooperating with what Jesus has already done for us. Lysa realizes that her ability to forgive others is not solely dependent on her determination or efforts but on leaning into Jesus' grace and allowing it to flow through her. She acknowledges that humans tend to hide in darkness, not only when they sin but also when they react to others' wrongdoings. However, God has provided a way for forgiveness that doesn't rely on our strength but on His forgiveness and redemption. By cooperating with His work, you can experience true forgiveness and freedom.

Forgiveness is a powerful act that brings forth the stunning revelation of Jesus in our lives. However, it's important to distinguish between redemption and reconciliation. Reconciliation requires the willingness of both parties to do the work to come back together, while redemption is a personal journey between you and God. Forgiveness doesn't always result in restored relationships, but it frees us to move forward and experience the beauty of life. Letting go of the desire for payback or suffering allows us to embrace the freedom God offers. As we scatter seeds of forgiveness, the muddy pit of pain transforms into fertile soil where beautiful things can grow. It's a gradual process that may still involve tears but ultimately leads to compassion instead of bitterness. Cooperating with forgiveness enables us to dance freely in the beauty of redemption. Taking time, understanding, insight, divine intervention, and openness are all essential in the journey toward forgiveness. We can navigate this process together, allowing space for personal revelations to emerge.

Key Points

- Lysa's marriage devastation caused her to seek refuge in sleep and hope for daily improvements while being plagued by anxiety, panic attacks, and overwhelming pain.

- The weight of her experiences led to the emergence of negative emotions like cynicism, bitterness, resentment, delay, and trust issues, creating a battle against forgiveness.

- Lysa realized the power of forgiveness and the importance of making choices to move forward, guided by grace, and fueled by God's truth.

- Forgiveness is a complex concept that requires cooperation with the grace provided by Jesus, allowing true forgiveness and freedom to emerge.

- Forgiveness is a transformative act that can lead to the revelation of Jesus in our lives, enabling us to let go of the desire for payback and experience the beauty of life, even if reconciliation may not always be possible.

Milestone Goals

- Are you currently in a situation where you are finding it difficult to forgive someone?

_____
_____
_____

- Have you had past incidents where due to your unforgiving nature, you missed out on the beauty of life, just like Lysa missed out on a fun day at the beach?

_____
_____
_____

- Have you noticed yourself battling the soldiers of unforgiveness?

_____
_____
_____

- Are you ready to understand the power of forgiveness and its connection to grace and God's truth?

_____

_____

_____

- What is the difference between redemption and reconciliation, and how does forgiveness play a role in both?

_____

_____

_____

Action Plan

- Identify if you have gradually turned into someone you cannot recognize. You may notice that you are bitter, resentful, and constantly looking for an escape from reality through sleep. Open your mind to the possibility of healing.

_____

_____

_____

- If you are currently not going through an incident, think of a past incident that you couldn't take your mind off due to your unforgiveness.

_____

_____

_____

- Enable Jesus to shower his grace through you. Prepare yourself to let him do his miracles on you.

_____

_____

_____

- Understand that redemption does not mean reconciliation. You are not being forced to rekindle relationships you don't want to.

_____

_____

_____

- Know that the journey is going to be hard but at the end it will free you of bitterness and give you peace.

_____

_____

_____

- Write down everything you learned in this chapter and compare it to what you already knew before

_____

_____

_____

Chapter 2 – Welcome to the Table

In the midst of writing this book, sitting at her gray wooden table, Lysa shared her experiences, struggles, and reflections on forgiveness. Some days were spent alone with her computer, tears, Bible, and personal battles with forgiveness. On other days, she invited friends to join her, creating a safe space for them to bring up their own life experiences to the table. One had unresolved feelings towards an ex that she'd thought she'd gotten over but seeing him get engaged aroused all of that past bitterness. One had a long-lost friend whose life decisions made their friendship wither away. Another was still in shock at the loss of her college-age cousin who was murdered. All of these experiences made Lysa realize that every single person has their own unique reactions and hesitations when it comes to forgiveness. Forgiveness can be a complex and difficult topic to navigate. However, throughout this process, she realized that life continues to present opportunities for forgiveness, even in the face of new challenges.

It is only natural to feel fear, hesitancy, anger, confusion, defeat, and frustration that can arise when considering forgiveness. There are many reasons that hold one back from forgiving, such as the fear of repeated offenses, the desire for control, the longing for validation, the challenge of forgiving when still harboring hostile feelings, and avoiding thinking of the incident altogether. Forgiving can seem weak and mellow, like letting the wrongdoer off the hook. However, that is not the case. Forgiveness is a major part of the Christian faith, but nobody quite understood how to forgive. Christians know that God commands it, but how do we do it? Lysa deeply studied the bible to find answers to this. She found that forgiveness is certainly God's command, but it is not cruel. It isn't to force us to forgive any wrongdoers. It is to God's divine mercy for human hearts that are so prone to turning hurt into hate. This does not mean that abuse should be tolerated and forgiven so easily. There are consequences for extreme actions such as brutal murder however, God invites us to forgive in such cases as well, although keeping in mind that God's mercy is not void of His justice.

The notion of "forgive and forget" is so often brought up however, the bible does not mention forgetting. It encourages us to forgive even without forgetting. We need to admit that some experiences we've had are not easy to forget, nor do we have to. We can always keep the good memories alive; hence, forgetting per se is unnecessary. What is important is to forgive.

Lysa pointed out her own journey of healing and the tendency to deny pain by adopting coping mechanisms or a facade of positivity. It is vital to confront one's reality honestly and engage in the hard work of healing, rather than thinking about what 'could've been'. As 'unhealed hurt becomes unleashed hurt spewed out on others'. Forgiveness should not be taken as a burden or an unrealistic expectation, but rather a transformative process that leads to freedom and a deeper understanding of God's mercy. In a world where hurt and offense are commonplace, forgiveness often goes against the norm. However, there's a powerful impact of someone choosing to forgive, surpassing the fleshly reactions of anger and resentment. Witnessing such forgiveness becomes a profound testament to the reality of God's work in the lives of individuals and communities.

Key Points

- Lysa shared her experiences, struggles, and reflections on forgiveness while writing her book with her friend circle whom all came together at her 'gray table'. She created a judgment-free zone to talk about the prevailing problems of her friends.

- She recognized that forgiveness can be complex and difficult, with unique reactions and hesitations for each individual.

- Lysa delved into studying the Bible to understand forgiveness and discovered that it is a command rooted in God's divine mercy.

- The idea of "forgive and forget" is not explicitly mentioned in the Bible; forgiveness is encouraged even without forgetting past experiences.

- Forgiveness is a transformative process that leads to freedom and a deeper understanding of God's mercy, and choosing to forgive has a profound impact on individuals and communities.

Milestone Goals

- What are the reasons you feel that causes one to be unforgiving?

_____

_____

_____

- Do you feel like forgiving is weak?

_____

_____

_____

- Are you prepared to accept that forgiveness is God's command?

_____

_____

_____

- Have you ever tried to forgive and forget? If so, how was the experience?

_____

_____

_____

Action Plan

- Understand that forgiveness is a complex and difficult concept to navigate. It takes a long process and hence be ready to take on a challenge.

_____

_____

_____

- Do not consider forgiveness as a weakness. It is God's command.

_____

_____

_____

- Understand that taking revenge is not a part of the Christian faith, but forgiving is. However, it does not mean that God turns a blind eye to the wrongdoers. His mercy is not void of justice.

_____

_____

_____

- Accept that you cannot forget certain incidents, however forgiving them is vital.

_____

_____

_____

- Realize that forgiveness is a transformative process that guides you to freedom and peace.

_____

_____

_____

Chapter 3 – Is This Even Survivable?

Forgiveness is a complex process that requires tireless effort. One morning, Lysa felt like she was finally making progress, ready to take on the day with hope however, within a few hours, she was triggered. Triggered by the painful memories that haunt her. She looked for a way to release her pain and slamming the front door seemed the best way to do it. As she was slamming the door screaming and flailing her arms about, she noticed a delivery girl staring at her in utter shock and fear. This was a turning point in her journey. She realized that she is hurting the people around her by hanging onto the pain. But how do you get over it? As the Bible says, 'forgive and you will be forgiven', yet it can seem impossible to apply it to your situation.

It is only natural that you want your wrongdoer to acknowledge your pain and do everything to make it right however, that only gives power to them over you. Forgiveness is a long way to go but the first step should be taking control of your emotions. What they did to you is beyond your control, but you *can* control how you feel about it. They've already done the damage but now you need to take control of your feelings and say *enough*. Acknowledge your pain. Own it. Blaming is easy and seems like the right thing to do however, you cannot sit around waiting for someone else to make you feel better. You are your own healer of the pain. This thought will free you from feeling powerless; powerless to change, powerless to heal.

The hopeless pursuit of expecting the other person to make things right is what rips you away from the hope-filled possibilities of tomorrow. Hope is where the healing begins. Just like the time markings of BC: Before Crisis and AD: After Devastation, there is a third and that is RH: Resurrected Hope. If you take the actual time markings of the present, it is 2023 years after Christ's death however, his death isn't what has carried us into so far in the future but His resurrected hope. This newfound hope will change your perspective. You will start seeing what you want to see. And what you see will start becoming your reality. Have you noticed that once you set your mind on buying a car you like, you start seeing that car often? It's not that suddenly the amount of people who bought that car increased but rather, you've started to notice them more. They've always been there. Likewise, Lysa realized that a new perspective will eventually turn into her reality, as she started seeing what she wanted more and more. She realized that to find this hope and see life's beauty again, she needs to go back to the place she lost hope. To the place where forgiveness felt cruel, and beauty faded.

Key Points

- Lysa experienced a turning point in her journey when she realized the impact of her pain on others and the need to release it.

- Forgiveness requires taking control of emotions and acknowledging personal responsibility for healing.

- Expecting others to make things right keeps one from finding hope and healing.

- Lysa discovered the power of hope in changing perspectives and shaping one's reality.

- To find hope and experience beauty again, she must confront the place where forgiveness felt cruel, and hope was lost.

Milestone Goals

- Have you ever found yourself unintentionally hurting those around you since you are bitter?

_____

_____

_____

- Have you expected your wrongdoers to realize their mistakes and do everything they can to make it right?

_____

_____

_____

- Whenever they have not risen to your expectations of redemption, do you feel powerless since you are waiting around for others to heal you?

_____

_____

_____

- Are you prepared to change your perspective and try to see the beauty of life again?

_____

_____

_____

Action Plan

- Understand that holding onto your pain only makes you bitter and you will end up hurting your loved ones around you.

_____

_____

_____

- Take personal responsibility for your own healing without waiting around for anyone to heal you. This will take the power away from them and give power to you.

_____

_____

_____

- Open yourself to a new reality by changing your perspective. This will resurrect your hope and you will be able to see beauty in life again.

_____

_____

_____

- Understand that to have this new-found hope, you need to go back to where you lost it. Healing starts at the root.

Chapter 4 – How is Forgiveness Even Possible When I Feel Like This?

During her journey to recovery, Lysa was sitting in her counselor's office, unmotivated to talk and ready to cry. She had scrambled to a point where she had not washed her hair in days, jeopardizing her personal hygiene and well-being. She did not feel like talking about her problems, let alone forgive anyone. She was hell-bent on making the people involved realize their mistakes, waiting for justice so that she felt like the situation has served both ends fairly and only then was she ready to consider forgiveness. However, as she spent time with her counselor, she realized that no amount of repentance from the wrongdoers can make this all go away. The damage will still be here, the hurt will still linger. She realized that it is vital to separate her healing from their choices.

You need to understand that your ability to heal cannot depend on anyone's choices but your own. You need to choose to heal and be open to the Lord to do his wonders. In the book of John, there are only two mentions of healing miracles performed by Jesus. In both of them, the people were healed only when they chose to obey the Lord. There was a lame man who thought he needed the help of others to get to the pool of Bethesda, to be healed by its water. When Jesus asked him if he wanted to be healed, he did not say yes but rather gave an excuse that people were not helping him get to the water. It was fascinating that he was so focused on others and not the powers of Jesus. However, Jesus paid no heed and simply told the man to rise. Instantly the man was healed. In the other miracle, Jesus did not want to know who made the man blind so that they could be blamed. Rather, he applied mud on his eyes and healed him. These miracles show how Jesus healed those who *want* to be healed, and not the ones who linger around, blaming others. Likewise, the ultimate truth is that your healing is *your* choice.

A necessary step towards healing is forgiveness. You need to stop yourself from replaying the incident in your head over and over again and to do this, you need to be able to forgive the person and escape the grip of the trauma. You need to place your trust in Jesus that He will equip you with all that is needed to forgive someone. He will give you the strength, courage, will, and everything in between. Refusing to forgive is refusing God's peace. Lysa's counselor gave her some cards and told her to write down every feeling of hurt and then gave her pieces of red felt to cover those cards. He set them out to be Jesus's blood shed on the cross, which is the best example of His forgiveness.

Forgiveness is both a decision and a process. Making the decision to forgive shows your willingness to forgive the facts of the incident. Forgiving the aftermath of it; the damage it did to you, is a process that should be dealt with later. Every trauma has an initial effect and a long-term impact. Although you forgive the initial incident, it is very easy for long-term disappointment to turn into bitterness and hate. These triggers that creep up on you make the incident feel extremely present, rather than in the past. Dealing with them is the process of forgiving without which you cannot move forward. Life does not wait for anyone. Time will flow as usual and the best thing you can do is go forward and move on.

Lysa understood that the impact of emotional trauma will result in physical weakness as well, as her colon twisted and cut off the blood flow. Her doctor told her that her insides looked like it has been hit by a bus. With time, you will learn to differentiate between a feeling and your reaction to it. You will learn to take time to analyze a feeling, rather than hastily reacting to it. And along the way, you will feel compassion for your wrongdoers, lifting your burdens and feeling lighter in your heart. You will understand that the reason they hurt you is most likely because they were hurting inside as well, through the doings of others. This will not justify their actions, but it will help you feel compassion and move forward. You may also decide that the pain ends with you. People often project their trauma onto others, however, this pain that has been inflicted on you should not continue onto others. One more act of forgiveness makes this world a better place.

Key Points

- Lysa recognized that her healing and well-being are dependent on her own choices and not on the actions of others.

- Forgiveness is a necessary step towards healing, allowing one to escape the grip of trauma and stop replaying painful memories.

- Making the decision to forgive shows a willingness to let go of the facts of the incident, while the process of forgiving deals with the long-term impact and triggers associated with it.

- Time does not wait, and moving forward is essential for personal growth and progress.

- Developing compassion for wrongdoers helps lift the burden of hurt, understanding that their actions may stem from their own inner pain, and choosing to end the cycle of pain by not projecting it onto others.

Milestone Goals

- How does Lysa's realization that her healing and well-being are her own responsibility impact your perspective on forgiveness and personal growth?

_____

_____

_____

- What are your thoughts on the concept of forgiveness as both a decision and a process? How does this understanding align with your own experiences or beliefs about forgiveness?

_____

_____

_____

- Reflecting on Lysa's counselor's approach of using cards and red felt as symbols of forgiveness, how do you think visual representations can aid in the process of forgiveness and healing? Can you think of any other creative methods that might be helpful in this context?

_____

_____

_____

- Discuss the significance of choosing to forgive
  despite the long-term impact and triggers
  associated with past trauma. How can one
  effectively navigate the process of forgiving
  without suppressing or ignoring the ongoing effects
  of the hurt?

_____

_____

_____

- How does the idea of compassion for wrongdoers
  resonate with you? Do you believe that
  understanding and compassion can coexist with
  holding individuals accountable for their actions?
  Share your thoughts on the potential role of
  compassion in breaking the cycle of pain and
  fostering personal growth.

_____

_____

_____

Action Plan

- Choose to heal. Without this choice, even God
  cannot heal you. Open your heart to let him in.

_____

_____

_____

- Stop yourself from replaying the incident over and over again.

_____

_____

_____

- Understand that forgiveness is both a decision and a process. Your decision to forgive will enable you to forgive the facts of the incident and then forgiving the long-lasting impact will be a process.

_____

_____

_____

- Realize that they hurt you because they were hurting as well. Decide that the pain ends with you and that you will not spread the hurt to others around you.

_____

_____

_____

Chapter 5 – Collecting the Dots

Lysa's incident with her husband Art, shattered her emotional safety net that had provided security for years. She had a belief that kept her guarded from men, but he was an exception. Whenever life threw something hard at her, she'd console herself by telling herself that at least her marriage was safe and secure. This is why the affair had a major impact on her life. She became uncertain about her beliefs and the way forward. Lysa recognized the importance of revisiting the past and understanding how past experiences shape present beliefs and actions and she shared her personal story.

Lysa's mother was a great influence in her life, she was 'her person'. They were more than just mother and daughter, but best friends and companions. Her mother was a free spirit, who was raised very lovingly by her grandparents and two aunts since her mother did not claim her and left her at a very young age. Having married a man in the military right after high school, she moved into the trailer next to her husband's parents' trailer. As he was deployed for most of Lysa's childhood, she and her mother were always alone, going through life's struggles together. This made them very close, sharing everything like the best of friends. Lysa knew no rules while growing up. The only rules were put by her grandmother i.e., her father's mother, who was obsessed with keeping things clean. She often made Lysa sit on a blanket while eating crackers and told her to lick the ends of the cracker after taking a bite so that no crumbs would fall.

Lysa's rule-free childhood came to an end when her sister Angee was born. 'Be nice to the baby, let her go first, be gentle, don't speak loud so the baby won't wake' etc. were all the new rules she now had to follow. However, her mother made sure there was no bitterness between the sisters and soon, the three of them became a tight-knit team. Lysa's father was a strict man who did not seem to bother about much of his kids' matters. When her mother got a parking ticket, he used the money that they had saved up for the county fair and said he wasn't taking them this year. She muttered a word she wasn't supposed to use under her breath, for her father and forever felt guilty about it. This day is when she understood the unfairness of life. As time flew by, their estranged grandmother i.e., her mother's mother rekindled their relationship. Whenever Lysa and her sister went to visit her, she would leave them with her neighbor to babysit them and he sexually abused her, threatening to hurt her mother if she ever told anyone. As a young nine-year-old who loved her mother, she was afraid of him and kept quiet. She also believed that she was a bad person as she said a bad word about her father and had stolen bubblegum at the convenience store. She started believing that she was at fault as she broke the rules and that she was being punished and vowed to become a better person. Her father left them soon after, and she never got to tell him what happened. When she was in middle school, one day she mustered up the courage and told her mom about it who eventually told her dad. She thought this would result in him rushing back to them, to protect them, but he never came. She felt very let down by her own father. However, her mother confronted the abusive neighbor and fought for Lys, yet again proving to be her person.

Her mother made it a point to teach the importance of forgiveness from a young age. Whenever Lysa and Angee would fight, she would intervene, get the wrongdoer to apologize, and make the other say "I forgive you" and hug it out. This was the process she knew whenever one hurt the other. The authoritative figure taking charge and making amends. In fifth grade, when her own friends betrayed her and made fun of her to join the popular girls, she naturally ran to her teacher, expecting her to make amends. Her teacher paid no attention but rather told her to stop being so emotional. Lysa was devastated. She was learning each day how people let her down, and how nothing happens to bad people and injustice prevails. She wanted people to own up to their mistakes and be kind to her, loving her for who she was. As this did not happen, she started becoming someone who plotted revenge. Lysa became the teacher's assistant so that she could look into her classmates' files and find bad things about them so that she can reveal them all to the 'judge' who would finally establish justice. She never found the judge she was looking for. She realized that the greatest hell here on earth is not suffering but feeling like the suffering is pointless and never-ending. Instead of playing fair, she realized that we all become what we swore to not become: mean kids. If you weren't mean at first, it will only take a few days of targeting to become mean. It felt safer to fit into the meanness than to be vulnerable. Later, you eventually become silent, emotionless, and distant, since you ultimately do not want to join the meanness, nor do you feel happiness. The disappointment drives you to become silent.

All of these childhood traumas shaped Lysa into who she was, and they impacted her journey toward forgiveness in the face of her present dilemma.

Key Points

- Lysa's incident with her husband shattered her emotional safety net, leading her to question her beliefs and the way forward.

- Her childhood experiences, including a close bond with her mother and traumatic events, shaped her perspective on forgiveness and justice.

- Lysa realized the importance of revisiting the past and understanding how past experiences impact present beliefs and actions.

- Her mother taught her the importance of forgiveness from a young age, but she struggled with feeling let down by others and seeking justice.

- Lysa's journey toward forgiveness is influenced by her childhood traumas and the need to heal and find a sense of purpose and meaning.

Milestone Goals

- Are there aware of any of your childhood traumas that may have shaped the person you are today?

_____

_____

_____

- Have you felt like everyone disappoints you in life?

_____

_____

_____

- Has your household taught you the importance of forgiveness from a young age?

_____

_____

_____

- Do you have a close person who you call 'my person'?

_____

_____

_____

Action Plan

- Understand that your present triggers are based on childhood traumas. Try to think of any incidents in your past.

_____

_____

_____

- Carefully set out your flow of thought in those situations. Did you feel sad, disappointed, let down, angry, frustrated, etc.?

_____

_____

_____

- If you have a family member who is very dear to you, get their help to identify any traumas.

_____
_____
_____

- Realize that these incidents have been holding you back.

_____
_____
_____

Chapter 6 – Connecting the Dots

Lysa shared her thoughts on the impact of the previous chapter with both her friend and husband. Her friend acknowledged the potential for messy but necessary conversations that will arise from reminiscing on the past, recognizing that such discussions are essential for personal growth and understanding. Lysa understood the importance of connecting past experiences to current beliefs and behaviors, suggesting that it is through this exploration that individuals can gain insights into their own actions and choices.

Having overheard her conversation with her friend, Art became emotional, tearing up and praising Lysa for her amazing writing. She was surprised to see him cry, as it was a very rare sight. Art was never taught to express emotion. Since childhood, his household taught him that emotions should be kept to oneself and not be expressed. On the contrary, Lysa's household was extremely expressive. Since Art was always silent, she never assumed he was under pressure or having any sort of problems. She thought everything was fine. During the beginning of their relationship, she did try to connect with him. She wanted something *more*, but she didn't exactly know what she was looking for. She couldn't put a finger on the 'more'. It was apparent that both she and Art have been influenced by their respective upbringings, leading to certain patterns and behaviors within their relationship. These patterns may not necessarily be healthy or conducive to true intimacy.

After the incident, Lysa realized what they had been lacking. It was *vulnerability*. Letting yourself be vulnerable doesn't necessarily mean letting yourself be hurt. It simply means becoming true to yourself. Self-awareness plays a major role in vulnerability. The more you don't pretend, the easier it will become to forgive your past traumas and move forward. Looking at the bible, Adam and Eve were completely naked yet had no shame. They knew they were made by God and their trust in Him made them fearless of vulnerability. Likewise, it was important to feel accepted and acceptable. To create a safe space completely void of shame and judgment, but that's empowering to grow. This vulnerability includes acknowledging and accepting past mistakes and flaws, allowing for growth and forgiveness within the relationship. True love involves seeing and accepting one another's imperfections while still recognizing each other's worth and potential. Lysa started seeing Art for more than what he did. His mistakes were not his identity, there was much more to that man. She began seeing him as a child of God, just like Adam, who is worthy of forgiveness and understanding.

Despite the progress, Lysa was still grieving. Grief is often connected with loss. You might think loss is always bad, but is it? God took a bone from Adam to create Eve. He gave him more than what he took away. Likewise, what if we consider loss as something that completes us? Makes us better aware of ourselves. Loss doesn't always have to be detrimental. Think of something you continuously dislike but don't know the exact reason for it. It could be a particular time of day, season, holiday, etc. Think back to any incident associated with it. Somewhere in your memory, you'll be able to dig out the exact reason for your dislike of it. Rather than avoiding it, intentionally work to reclaim your liking towards it.

Lysa's friend used to hate sunrises and sunsets for no apparent reason. As she jogged her memory, she realized that this time of day is when she felt most threatened during her circumstances as a child. Although she has not experienced such circumstances in over thirty years, she still had not healed from it. She finally found herself enjoying a sunset when visiting a friend in another state as she considered it to be different from home, only to find out it was the same sunset. That is when she finally decided to let go of her resentment for sunsets.

We can't change what we have experienced but we can choose how the experience changes us. It is totally worth taking control of your emotions and reclaiming them. And whenever you don't feel like you can forgive or make it through your hard times, have faith in God.

Key Points

- Lysa realizes the importance of discussing past experiences and connecting them to present beliefs for personal growth and understanding.

- Art's emotional reaction to Lysa's writing highlights the impact of his upbringing on his ability to express emotions and connect with others.

- Lysa and Art's relationship patterns are influenced by their respective upbringings, which may hinder true intimacy and vulnerability.

- Lysa recognizes the significance of vulnerability and self-awareness in forgiving past traumas and fostering a safe space within the relationship.

- Lysa and her friend's experiences with grief and reclaiming lost preferences demonstrate the potential for growth and healing in embracing past losses and choosing how experiences shape them.

Milestone Goals

- How do you think past experiences and upbringing can influence patterns and behaviors within relationships?

_____
_____
_____

- How does vulnerability contribute to forgiveness and personal growth in the context of healing from past traumas?

_____
_____
_____

- What are some strategies or practices that can help individuals embrace vulnerability and create a safe space within their relationships?

_____
_____
_____

- How can the process of grief and reevaluating our dislikes or aversions lead to personal growth and a shift in perspective?

_____
_____
_____

Action Plan

- Understand the parameters of expressing emotion that you learned from childhood. Realize if your household hides feelings or openly expresses them.

_____
_____
_____

- If your partner or loved is silent, do not assume they are fine. Understand that sometimes the silent ones are the ones most in pain. Talk to them.

_____
_____
_____

- Open yourself to becoming vulnerable. Vulnerability will let you and your loved ones connect on a deeper level.

_____
_____
_____

- Create a judgment-free environment so that you can freely express emotions.

_____

_____

_____

- Understand that loss isn't always bad. It teaches you a lesson nothing else could. God had a bigger plan for you and will give something better for what he took away.

_____

_____

_____

Chapter 7 – Correcting the Dots

Lysa sat at the gray table, contemplating the importance of connecting the dots in her life. She realized that merely collecting the dots was not enough; she needed to go a step further and correct the dots. She understood that the perceptions and beliefs she formed based on her experiences could either be life-giving or toxic and it is vital to investigate the toxic perceptions.

Look at individuals who personalize everything, filtering every word and action through unresolved pain and unhealed hurts from their past. These individuals would quickly assign wrong motives and negative interpretations to what others said or did. They believed that they were disliked, not smart enough, unwanted, and constantly attacked. Soon enough, their perceptions tainted their relationships and made others feel exhausted and misunderstood.

This is why forgiveness and understanding the roots of your pain are essential. It is always easier to identify the dots that needed correction in others, but harder to see them in yourself. This understanding prompted Lysa to write a chapter, a guide to help others identify toxic perceptions and beliefs hindering their path to healing. Drawing inspiration from the canary used as an early-warning detector in British coal mines, Lysa compared her chapter to a canary in a cage, guiding readers to sniff out unhealthy perceptions and beliefs. She emphasized the need to correct the dots and to process and transform your thoughts, feelings, and interpretations of your circumstances, relationships, and self.

Our experiences shape our perceptions, which in turn become our beliefs. These beliefs then influence what we see in the world. She used an example of seeing a dust bunny in the kitchen, which might be innocently ignored until a past experience with a mouse creates a perception that every speck of dust is a potential threat. Our emotional perceptions work similarly, shaping our interpretations of reality. If you collected dots and made connections in your own stories, your perceptions might start to shift. Correcting the dots required time, pain, acceptance, and perspective.

To correct the dots, think of this example. Notice the reactions and physical and emotional responses when thinking about certain individuals. Do you feel resentment, vindictiveness, or judgment? Can you find peace, pray for them, and offer helpful perspectives? She emphasized the importance of reframing the story, finding redeeming qualities, and considering the lessons learned.

Throughout the journey of correcting the dots, she stressed that it was not a linear or straightforward process. Be honest with your feelings and thoughts, challenge distorted thinking, seek counsel from trusted friends and professionals, and apply the truth of God's Word to your perceptions.

Healing and finding healthy perspectives would take time and should not be rushed. Embrace your emotions, process your thoughts, and be present in the journey. You can use this personal declaration:

1. I DON'T NEED TO RUN AWAY. What I'm looking for will never be found somewhere out there.

2. I DON'T NEED TO ISOLATE. Lies scream loudest when there are no other voices to call foul.

3. I DON'T NEED TO NUMB IT AWAY. Avoiding feelings will not help, rather addressing them will. When feelings are properly addressed, it paves the way for peace, hope, and healing.

4. I DON'T NEED TO SILENCE MY JOURNALED WORDS. The words I'm writing are putting my heart on display. It will help listen to what it needs.

5. THERE IS A HEALED VERSION OF ME THAT IS WAITING AND WANTING TO EMERGE. I will reject the seduction of nursing my grudges by revisiting old proof over and over, that only reminds me of the incident. I have collected, connected, and corrected the dots and now I trust in God's most merciful outcome, that I'm living right now. I'm not a victim. I'm a healed woman walking in victory.

This served as a beacon of hope and guidance for readers on their path to healing and forgiveness. It was a reminder that by correcting your perceptions and beliefs, you could transform your understanding of yourself, others, and the world. Your pain could be a gateway to growth, learning, and eventually helping others. With time, patience, and a commitment to self-reflection, you embarked on a journey of healing and discovery, ready to embrace a future filled with love, forgiveness, and hope.

Key Points

- Lysa realizes the importance of correcting toxic perceptions and beliefs in order to foster healing and healthy relationships.

- Our experiences shape our perceptions, which then become our beliefs and influence how we see the world.

- Correcting the dots requires time, pain, acceptance, and perspective, and it is not a linear or straightforward process.

- Strategies for correcting toxic perceptions include reframing stories, finding redeeming qualities in others, and seeking counsel from trusted individuals.

- Embracing emotions, processing thoughts, and being present in the journey is essential for healing and discovering a future filled with love, forgiveness, and hope.

Milestone Goals

- How do our past experiences and unresolved pain shape our perceptions and beliefs about ourselves and others?

_____
_____
_____

- What are some strategies for identifying and correcting toxic perceptions and beliefs that hinder our healing and relationships?

_____

_____

_____

- How does reframing our stories and finding redeeming qualities in others contribute to a healthier perspective and forgiveness?

_____

_____

_____

- Why is it important to seek counsel and apply the truth of God's Word in the process of correcting our perceptions and beliefs?

_____

_____

_____

Action Plan

- Look into the beliefs you established in childhood. Correcting the dots requires you to eliminate toxic beliefs.

_____

_____

_____

- Pay attention to your triggers. This will help you think back to past traumas and find the root cause of it.

_____

_____

_____

- Understand the importance of shifting your perspective once you correct your dots.

_____

_____

_____

- Embrace your emotions and feelings using a personal declaration. The sooner the face your emotions, the sooner you will find peace.

_____

_____

_____

Chapter 8 – Unchangeable Feel Unforgivable

In a small box tucked away in the attic, there lay the remnants of a childhood long forgotten. Among the mementos, there was a black-and-white photograph of a young girl leaning against a tree. This photo held more than just an image of a bygone era; it held the secrets of a painful past.

The girl in the picture had long brown hair, was kissed by the sun, and was tangled in messy ringlets. Her smooth skin and small body betrayed her innocence, but her eyes spoke of hidden sadness. In that season of her life, she endured unspeakable abuse at the hands of her grandmother's neighbor. He not only violated her body but also sought to destroy her mind and soul, using twisted interpretations of scriptures to convince her of her own wickedness.

The abuse stole more than just her innocence; it stole her freedom to be a carefree child. She learned to hide within herself, practicing the art of self-preservation. Even after the abuse ended, she carried the weight of fear, always expecting the worst to happen. While others assumed the best, she braced herself for impact, constantly living in anticipation of tragedy. As she grew older, she sought healing through counseling, but the aftereffects of her childhood trauma lingered. Her mind was wired to jump to extremes, imagining a thousand different worst-case scenarios. She planned for funerals and worried endlessly, unable to let go of the fear that had become ingrained in her thinking.

She longed for a life where she could simply enjoy herself without the constant apprehension. Yet, her experiences seemed to defy statistical probability, as if hard and unfair things were destined to happen to her. She carried the weight of grief for the losses she had endured—the loss of her baby sister, her father's absence, the tragic car accidents, and the betrayals that scarred her deeply.

Forgiveness seemed unfathomable in the face of such pain and loss. How could she forgive those who had hurt her so deeply? And what purpose would it serve if they were no longer present or willing to cooperate? These questions plagued her as she wrestled with the concept of forgiveness.

But through her journey, she discovered a few truths that helped her navigate the path toward forgiveness. She realized that:

1. Forgiveness was more satisfying than revenge - Seeking revenge only added to her own pain and suffering, while forgiveness released her need for others to be punished. It placed the offenders in God's hands, allowing her to soften her heart and desire peace instead of retaliation.

2. God is not a do-nothing God - Even in the midst of her pain, she found comfort in knowing that God was always working, even if she couldn't see it. She looked to the story of Joseph, who endured years of hardship but ultimately saw God's plan unfold, through helping save millions of lives during a famine. Though she may not fully understand how God was working in her own painful experiences,

she held onto the belief that He was faithful and had a purpose.

3. Her offenders were also suffering from their own pain - Compassion became the key to forgiveness. Instead of harboring anger and resentment, she chose to have compassion for the wounds that led them to make hurtful choices. Understanding that they too carried their own burdens of pain helped soften her heart and find empathy for their brokenness.

4. The purpose of forgiveness is not always reconciliation – She did not have to go back to the people who hurt her and rekindle a relationship. Forgiveness is for herself, not for others. It does not mean trust is immediately restored but rather having her heart at peace.

5. The enemy is the real villain – The devil works its way into our lives by creating barriers between humans. God has instructed us to beware of the devil's schemes.

In her journey toward forgiveness, she discovered that it wasn't just about letting go of the past; it was about finding peace within herself. It was about reclaiming her joy and refusing to let the wounds define her. Forgiveness was a process, and though it was difficult, she knew it was the only way to break free from the chains of bitterness and resentment.

As she placed the photograph back in the box, she felt a sense of release. The little girl in the picture no longer was the cautious girl ripped from her childhood. She was a child of God who gladly walked on his path to forgiveness and was a proud survivor.

Key Points

- Lysa's childhood abuse and traumatic experiences left her carrying the weight of fear and trauma into adulthood.

- Forgiveness seemed unfathomable due to the pain and loss she had endured, and she struggled to understand its purpose.

- Through her journey, she learned that forgiveness is more satisfying than revenge, releasing the need for punishment and fostering peace within oneself.

- She found solace in the belief that God is always working, even in the midst of pain, and that there is a greater purpose behind her experiences.

- Compassion for the offenders' own pain and brokenness helped soften her heart and enabled her to find empathy, leading to a path of forgiveness and self-healing.

Milestone Goals

- Have you ever experienced a situation where you found it challenging to forgive someone? How did that experience impact you and your relationships?

———————————————————————
———————————————————————
———————————————————————

- How do you think childhood experiences, particularly traumatic ones, can shape a person's perception of themselves and the world? Can you recall any instances where past experiences influenced your beliefs or behaviors?

_____

_____

_____

- Reflecting on the story, what are your thoughts on the connection between empathy, compassion, and forgiveness? Do you believe it's possible to forgive someone without understanding their pain or perspective?

_____

_____

_____

- How does your personal belief system or faith, if applicable, influence your understanding of forgiveness and its role in healing and moving forward?

_____

_____

_____

- Are there any past hurts or resentments that you feel are weighing you down? What steps could you take to begin the process of forgiveness and finding peace within yourself?

_____

_____

_____

Action Plan

- Think of an incident that hurt you badly. Yes, it will be difficult, but prepare yourself to forgive the person associated with it.

  _____

  _____

  _____

- Accept that forgiveness is better than revenge. Trust in God to do his part in bringing you peace and happiness.

  _____

  _____

  _____

- Be compassionate. Your offenders are also going through pain of their own.

  _____

  _____

  _____

- Understand that reconciliation is not necessary, you are simply forgiving someone for their acts. They don't have to be welcomed back into your life.

_____

_____

_____

- Identify the real villain who is the devil. He who tries to come between you and God is the real villain.

_____

_____

_____

Chapter 9 – Boundaries That Help Us Stop Dancing With Dysfunction

In the pouring rain, Lysa found herself driving home, feeling helpless and devastated. Art's affair was a destructive choice, and the consequences were affecting both of their lives. She realized that she was as powerless to fix this situation as she was to stop the rain. She couldn't control things that were beyond her control.

The choices made by Art not only hurt her emotionally but also caused her financial and mental distress. It felt like her dreams and hopes for the future were being flushed away. Forgiveness became complicated in this situation because the person she loved was intentionally causing harm, and she felt powerless to stop it. She was caught between wanting to forgive and the reality of the ongoing damage.

She acknowledged that when someone made destructive choices, it was usually because they were hurting themselves. She could choose to invest her energy in two directions: setting appropriate boundaries or trying to change the person. Trying to change someone who didn't want to change only led to frustration and disappointment. You put in all your effort to save this person however, if they don't want to be saved, your efforts go to waste.

Drawing boundaries is essential to protect yourself from the consequences of their actions. She shared her personal struggle with wanting to rescue the person she cared about but realizing that true change could only come from within. She had to shift from *efforts of control* to *efforts of compassion*, loving the person and empathizing with their pain while acknowledging her own limitations.

Enabling the destructive behavior was not an act of love. Enabling could take various forms, such as covering up their choices, rescuing them from consequences, or defending and rationalizing their actions. Forgiveness should not have been a justification for allowing someone to continue harming themselves or others. Boundaries are necessary to protect yourself and maintain accountability. Boundaries don't mean you completely push people away or cut them off, but rather hold yourself together. It's important for people to understand that you have forgiven them, however, it does not mean they can go back to their old ways. If they do, your boundaries will prevent them from bringing any negativity back into your life.

Lysa brought in the biblical perspective of love, highlighting Romans 12:15, which encouraged weeping with and rejoicing with others. However, amidst the rain and the pain, she realized that she couldn't control the choices of her loved one. She could offer support and love, but ultimately, the decision to change lay with the person themselves.

When setting boundaries, think to yourself, "What sort of person do I want to be? What time periods do I have limited capacity or am I always available to people? Do I feel freedom in this relationship to communicate? What is the best time to communicate with them? What is not the best time? How am I suffering the consequences of their actions?" are some things you can think about. It is vital that you set them for your sanity, and it is even more vital to stay consistent with them for the sake of stability.

Remember these when setting boundaries:

1. State your boundaries clearly and do not negotiate excuses.

2. Mute someone's unhealthy reaction. You can easily do this on social media.

3. Do not sweep lies under the rug and cover up others' mistakes. Clearly communicate that such behavior will diminish your trust.

4. You can always say no. You don't have to be available to please others.

5. Be honest with what you can and cannot give. Communicating your capacity sets consistent expectations.

6. If you feel like they are continuously having a negative impact on your mood, limit their access to your vulnerable moments.

7. Choose not to engage in conversations that take you down the unpleasant memory lane. Speaking to professionals is encouraged but anyone else who only wants the juicy details should be avoided.

8. Do not crumble if the other person accuses you of wrong intentions when you set boundaries. Explain the importance of them.

As she drove through the rain, her heart heavy with the weight of the situation, she found solace in the knowledge that she could control her own actions and responses. She could choose to set healthy boundaries, protect herself, and offer love and support from a distance. And as the rain continued to fall, she found strength in her own resilience and the hope that one day, her loved one might find the strength to change.

Key Points

- Lysa grapples with the devastating consequences of her partner's destructive choices, which affect her emotionally, financially, and mentally.

- Forgiveness becomes complex when the person causing harm is someone she loves deeply, and she struggles with the tension between wanting to forgive and the ongoing damage being done.

- She realizes that true change can only come from within the person making destructive choices, and her role shifts from trying to change them to setting appropriate boundaries for her own well-being.

- Enabling destructive behavior is not an act of love, and she emphasizes the importance of maintaining boundaries to protect herself and hold others accountable.

- She highlights the need to prioritize her own mental and emotional health by setting clear boundaries, being honest about her capacity, and avoiding engaging in conversations or situations that negatively impact her well-being.

Milestone Goals

- Have you ever felt powerless in a situation where someone's destructive choices were affecting your life? How did you handle it?

_____

_____

_____

- Do you think it's possible to love someone and set boundaries at the same time? Why or why not?

_____

_____

_____

- Have you ever found yourself enabling someone's harmful behavior? How did it impact your own well-being?

_____

_____

_____

- How do you prioritize your own mental and emotional health when dealing with difficult relationships?

_____

_____

_____

- What strategies or techniques do you use to communicate and establish boundaries effectively?

_____
_____
_____

Action Plan

- Accept that you change or control what happened. All you can do is control how you deal with it.

_____
_____
_____

- You cannot change someone who does not want to change. You need to set boundaries so that their actions do not harm you any further.

_____
_____
_____

- Understand that these boundaries are not set to push people away but rather to protect yourself from further damage.

_____
_____
_____

- Clearly communicate your boundaries and do not entertain anyone that does not respect them.

_____

_____

_____

- Maintaining these boundaries is key.

_____

_____

_____

Chapter 10 – Because They Thought God Would Save Them

In the midst of this season filled with chaos, pain, and destruction, Lysa found herself questioning the presence and power of God. She desperately sought His intervention and imagined countless scenarios in which He could miraculously fix everything. However, day after day, she saw no tangible evidence of God's intervention in her situation with Art. Feeling unseen and unheard, Lysa's faith began to falter.

Her prayers, once filled with hope and expectation, dwindled down to a single question: Why? The promises and statements she had believed in the past now felt empty and distant. Lysa struggled to hold onto hope, as it seemed risky and futile in the face of her circumstances. She yearned for clarity from God, longing for a clear direction to move forward.

One Saturday morning, Art surprised her by agreeing to attend a prayer service with her. Filled with hope, she believed that this could be the moment of breakthrough. As they sat in the sanctuary, Lysa noticed the texture of the gray seats and watched as Art lifted his hands in worship. Tears streamed down her face, convinced that God was about to move.

The pastor led the congregation through a message, and they were encouraged to pray for others while seeking personal breakthroughs. she hesitated, hoping Art would join her, but he remained still. She decided to go forward and picked up prayer cards, only to discover that they were written by men in prison, seeking prayer for their sons. Despite their differences, she understood the feeling of being trapped and unable to escape.

As the prayer service ended, she watched others leaving the church, envious of their seemingly normal lives. The miracle she had hoped for had not come to pass, and her heart was heavy with disappointment. They went out to breakfast, but she could barely eat. That night, she found herself curled up in the fetal position, overwhelmed by the emotional turmoil within her.

Amid her pain and confusion, Lysa questioned God's love and care. She felt betrayed, wondering why He seemed silent in her suffering. The darkness of her perspective began to overshadow her faith, causing her to doubt God's provision, protection, and instructions. Fear crept in, suggesting that perhaps there was no plan at all, and she was destined to be a victim of uncontrollable circumstances.

However, she knew deep within her heart that she could not escape the truth found in God's Word. She recognized that what she saw with her human eyes was not the entirety of what God was doing. Looking back on her life, she remembered times when God's faithfulness was evident, even if it unfolded gradually and subtly. His silence does not mean His absence. God works in silent and slow ways, that finally bring the necessary peace.

On one particularly stormy Sunday morning, she faced the choice of staying home or attending church alone on Sabbath day. Despite the resistance she felt, she chose to press through the storm and be reminded of God's faithfulness. She recognized that today was only part of the story, and she needed to be in a place where she could see beyond the present.

As Lysa persevered, she realized that her journey was not over. She learned to trust that God's timing is perfect and that His love for her remains steadfast. Though forgiveness and healing seemed uncertain, she held onto the hope that God was working, even when she couldn't see it. In her moments of doubt, she sought solace in the truth and sought reminders of God's faithfulness.

Key Points

- Lysa questions the presence and power of God amidst chaos and pain, feeling unseen and unheard in her desperate prayers for intervention.

- Her faith falters as she grapples with the absence of tangible evidence of God's intervention and struggles to hold onto hope in the face of her circumstances.

- Lysa experiences disappointment and doubt when a hoped-for breakthrough at a prayer service doesn't come to pass, leading her to question God's love and care.

- Despite her doubts, Lysa acknowledges that her perspective is limited and that God's faithfulness may unfold gradually and subtly, even in moments of silence.

- Lysa chooses to persevere, pressing through storms and seeking reminders of God's faithfulness, trusting in His perfect timing, and holding onto hope for forgiveness and healing.

Milestone Goals

- Have you ever questioned the presence and power of God in the midst of challenging circumstances? How did you navigate through your doubts?

  _____
  _____
  _____

- What does it mean to you to hold onto hope when you don't see tangible evidence of God's intervention in your life?

  _____
  _____
  _____

- Can you relate to Lysa's experience of disappointment and doubt when her prayers for a breakthrough weren't answered as she had hoped? How did you handle similar moments of disappointment in your own faith journey?

  _____
  _____
  _____

- How do you reconcile the idea of God's love and care with moments of silence or apparent absence in your life? How do you find reassurance in those times?

_____

_____

_____

Action Plan

- Understand that it is vital to not lose faith in God in these difficult times.

_____

_____

_____

- Believe that God has bigger plans and is working His miracles even when you feel like you are drowning.

_____

_____

_____

- Your perseverance is what will be rewarded. Having faith when nothing else seemed to go your way will finally bring you peace.

_____

_____

_____

Chapter 11 – Forgiving God

Lysa had experienced deep hurt and disillusionment in her life. She carried the weight of pain caused by people, and at times, she even questioned why God would allow such things to happen. Forgiving God seemed like an insurmountable task as she carried the heavy burden of unanswered questions and unresolved emotions.

Amid her emotional turmoil, a significant event unfolded within her large, close-knit family. They were all excited about embarking on a new business venture, but she couldn't muster the same enthusiasm. Instead, she felt intense fear and saw nothing but impending disaster. Convinced that God would intervene and prevent it, she prayed fervently, pouring out her concerns to both God and her family. She believed that obstacles would arise, rendering the whole idea impossible.

To her surprise, however, instead of God closing doors, it seemed as though He was opening them one after another. Her family's excitement grew with each passing day, while she withdrew further into her own anxieties. She struggled to see the potential good in the situation, desperately wanting her family to listen and understand her reservations. Her anxiety intensified, and her frustration turned into bitterness and anger.

In the midst of her confusion and despair, she sought solace in her journal. She poured her heart out, writing the word "confused" as a reflection of her state of mind. Suddenly, a phrase flashed across her consciousness: "This investment is an answered prayer." At first, she dismissed it, unable to fathom how the situation before her could possibly be an answer from God. However, the phrase persisted, gently nudging her to reconsider her perspective.

For over a week, she prayed earnestly for clarity, desperately seeking God's guidance. She asked Him to help her see this circumstance from a different angle, to shed light on the hidden blessings that might be present. Gradually, her heart began to soften, and her rigid stance started to crumble. She opened herself up to the possibility that her fears and doubts were clouding her judgment.

As she continued to pray and seek guidance, she started noticing small signs—a word of encouragement from a friend, a timely verse in the Bible, or a peaceful moment of reflection—that pointed her toward a new understanding. Slowly but surely, she began to see the investment opportunity in a different light. She recognized the passion and dedication in her family's eyes and realized that this venture was an expression of their love and unity.

With her heart transformed, she approached her family, not as an adversary, but as someone willing to listen and understand. They shared their dreams, hopes, and plans with her, and she reciprocated with genuine curiosity and support. In the process, she realized that her perspective had shifted, and the once-feared investment now seemed like an avenue for growth, connection, and even healing. She realized that she needed to place her trust in God as we only see what we can imagine but God is building something we cannot even fathom. Take Adam and Eve for example. They had placed their trust completely in

God's plan but as soon as they ate the fruit of the Tree of Knowledge of Good and Evil, they traded their eternal perspective for an imperfect earthly perspective. They started feeling shame and ran and hid, they had to leave the garden. Whenever you are in turmoil, shut out any arguments that come to mind against God. They are like the forbidden fruit that would push you away from eternal happiness. It's faith that will win all your battles.

Through her journey, Lysa learned that sometimes, the answers to our prayers come in unexpected forms. She discovered that God's wisdom surpasses our understanding and that He can use even the most unlikely situations to bring about healing and restoration. In embracing this newfound understanding, she found peace and renewed faith in the goodness of God's plans for her life.

Key Points

- Lysa carries the weight of pain and questions why God allows it, making it difficult for her to forgive Him.

- Despite her fears, Lysa's family embarks on a new business venture, and instead of obstacles, doors seem to open.

- Through journaling and prayer, Lysa begins to see the investment opportunity from a new perspective, guided by small signs and moments of reflection.

- Her heart transforms, and she approaches her family with curiosity and support, realizing the potential for growth, connection, and healing.

- Lysa learns that God's wisdom surpasses understanding, and unexpected situations can bring about healing and restoration, leading her to find peace and renewed faith.

Milestone Goals

- Have you ever struggled with forgiving God or questioning why certain things happen in your life? How did you work through those feelings?

_____
_____
_____

- Can you relate to Lysa's experience of feeling fearful and seeing only impending disaster, even when others around her were excited about a new opportunity? How do you typically handle moments of anxiety or doubt?

_____
_____
_____

- Have you ever had a situation where you felt a persistent nudge or phrase that challenged your perspective on a particular circumstance? How did you respond to it?

_____

_____

_____

- How do you seek clarity and guidance from God when you are faced with confusion or despair? Are there specific practices or habits that help you open yourself up to new perspectives?

_____

_____

_____

- Can you think of a time when you discovered hidden blessings or a new understanding in a situation that initially seemed challenging or undesirable? How did that experience impact your faith and trust in God's plans?

_____

_____

_____

Action Plan

- You will realize that you question everything that happens around you, as you feel like you have lost faith in God.

_____

_____

_____

- Pay attention to subtle signals sent by God that illuminates his grace toward you.

_____

_____

_____

- Prepare to see everything in a new light and realize that God has never left your side.

_____

_____

_____

- Understand that sometimes answers to your prayers come in unexpected forms.

_____

_____

_____

Chapter 12 – The Part That Loss Plays

Lysa attended a funeral, which made her think deeply about loss as a crucible that tests our strength immensely. It was a somber occasion, and she found herself much more emotional than she had anticipated. The young woman who had passed away had left this world unexpectedly, leaving behind a void that seemed impossible to fill. She couldn't help but wonder how such a vibrant and beautiful soul could suddenly cease to exist. The realization that she would never have another conversation with her friend again was heartbreaking.

She had always been deeply affected by the loss of others. Even if she didn't personally know the departed, she empathized with the pain of those who mourned. The sacred nature of grief touched her soul, connecting her with others who were going through the early devastations of loss. The tears shed by the ones who knew the departed seeped into her own emotions, merging their sorrow with her own.

But grief isn't always tied to the passing of a loved one. Sometimes, the pain came from being rejected by someone you loved. It is excruciating to experience the loss of a relationship, especially when the other person made the conscious choice to walk away. You not only grieve their absence but also their lack of concern for how their decision affected you. The anguish of being rejected by someone you cared for deeply, cuts through your heart.

The loss took many forms in Lysa's life. Whether it was someone leaving, moving away, or simply fading away, the emptiness created a phantom feeling. She would instinctively reach out to them, only to be reminded that they were no longer there. The longing for their presence became a constant ache, and the everyday moments they had shared together became precious memories tinged with sorrow. She understood that loss had a profound impact on her emotions. It was a crucible that pressed into the deepest parts of her being, causing pain that was often indescribable. The replays of past memories danced before her eyes, reminding her of the beauty that once existed in her life. However, those same replays brought tears to her eyes, for they served as a cruel reminder of what was lost.

Amidst the pain of loss, she discovered that sitting in grief could be a cure for bitterness. It seemed counterintuitive, but revisiting the depths of sorrow allowed her to confront her bitterness head-on. She realized that bitterness often found its way into her heart through the avenue of loss. But if loss was the cause, perhaps revisiting grief could pave the way for healing.

She acknowledged that bitterness didn't stem from hate but from deep hurt. It was a defense mechanism born out of the fear of being hurt again. Bitterness often took root in tender hearts, hearts that had been betrayed and wounded. It wasn't a reflection of her character but rather a sign that she had loved deeply and had been hurt deeply in return.

With this understanding, she saw bitterness in a different light. It wasn't a flaw or a mark of weakness but a response to pain. Softening the hardness of her heart and allowing the tears of grief to flow helped break up the hardened ground within her. Just as a farmer tills the soil to make it fertile, she recognized the importance of regularly tending to the hard places in her heart.

Attending the funeral had a profound impact on her. It served as a poignant reminder not to leave important words unsaid, and not to let differences or misunderstandings hinder relationships. She had allowed some disagreements to create distance between her and the young woman who had passed away, and she regretted not trying harder to maintain their connection.

Funerals, she realized, didn't have to be confined to a church ceremony with a casket present. Marked moments of grief occurred every day, and it was essential for her to honor those losses, both big and small. She made a promise to herself to be more present, to cherish the people in her life, and to express her love and appreciation before it was too late.

In the end, she understood that loss was an inevitable part of life. It was painful and challenging, but it also had the power to transform and heal. Through her experiences, she discovered the resilience of the human spirit and the capacity to find light in the darkest of times. She carried the memories of those she had lost in her heart, and their absence served as a constant reminder to live fully and love deeply.

Key Points

- Lysa attends a funeral and reflects on the profound impact of loss, both from the passing of loved ones and the pain of rejected relationships.

- Loss takes many forms in Lysa's life, leaving behind emptiness, longing, and bittersweet memories.

- She discovers that sitting in grief can be a cure for bitterness, allowing her to confront the deep hurt and soften her heart.

- Attending the funeral reminds Lysa to cherish relationships, express love, and not leave important words unsaid.

- Lysa recognizes that loss is a part of life, but it also has the power to transform and heal, leading her to live fully and love deeply.

Milestone Goals

- Have you ever experienced a significant loss in your life that deeply impacted you? How did you cope with it?

_____
_____
_____

- How do you personally relate to the idea that grief can be a crucible that tests our strength and transforms us?

_____
_____
_____

- In what ways have you seen bitterness manifest in your own life, and how have you dealt with it?

- How do you approach the topic of expressing love and appreciation to the people in your life? Do you have any regrets about not doing so?

- How do you find meaning and purpose in the face of loss and the inevitability of change?

Action Plan

- Realize how closely loss and grief are associated. Understand that grief doesn't only stem from the passing of a loved one but rather when they leave you as well.

- To overcome bitterness, reach deep down to the depths of the losses you experienced.

- Consider bitterness as a response to pain, not a weakness in you.

_____
_____
_____

- Cherish your loved ones as they may not be around forever, and cherish your relationships as well.

_____
_____
_____

Chapter 13 – Bitterness Is a Bad Deal That Makes Big Promises

During a busy day, she found herself holding a card in her hands. It was a birthday card, meant to convey love and celebration to someone who was no longer a part of her life. This person had been absent when she needed them the most, and their actions had left a deep sense of hurt within her. Yet, against her better judgment, she had decided to make an exception and send them this card.

Sitting across from Art at a dinner table, they contemplated the right words to write inside the card. They wanted to be kind and genuine in their sentiments. As they sealed the envelope and added extra postage, she couldn't help but feel a mix of emotions. She believed that sending the card was the right thing to do, a gesture of forgiveness and healing. Little did she know, the universe had other plans for testing her resolve.

Not long after, she received an email bearing frustrating news unrelated to the person who had received the card. It was a matter of someone not doing the job that she paid for, for which she was being billed excessively. The unfairness of it all overwhelmed her, igniting a fiery anger within that seemed disproportionate to the situation at hand. She yearned for justice, for someone to acknowledge the pain caused by these individuals who had hurt her before. The unresolved hurts from her past began to intertwine with the present, clouding her judgment and intensifying her emotions.

Her counselor, Jim, often reminded her that our reactions are reflections of our past hurts. At this moment, her reaction was hysterical, and it was undoubtedly historical. Bitterness had silently seeped into every corner of her being, corroding her peace and distorting her perspective. Even though the person she had sent the card to had no connection to the email she received, her bitter lens linked them together, amplifying her pain and frustration.

The weight of all her resentments and unhealed wounds pressed upon her relentlessly. It felt as if the world itself was against her, and she couldn't see a way out of this overwhelming despair. In her desperation, she turned to Art, needing him to defend her, to make everything right. It was then that he posed a question that struck at the heart of the matter.

"Are you angry because you haven't seen evidence of God defending you?" Art asked calmly, piercing through the chaos of her emotions. It was a moment of absolute clarity, forcing her to confront a bitter reality she had been avoiding. Yes, she was angry because she hadn't witnessed the reckoning she desired for those who had caused her pain. She questioned why God hadn't shown them the error of their ways and brought them to apologize.

Art gently suggested that perhaps their lack of acknowledgment wasn't evidence against God, but rather a reflection of their own journey. It was a perspective that challenged her to consider a different path—one of humility and surrender. The truth was, she couldn't control their actions or force them to apologize. What she could control was her own response and her own healing.

At that moment, she made a choice—an uncomfortable and humbling choice. She bowed low, offering her pain and resentment to God. She released her need for justice, for revenge, and for apologies. Instead, she asked Him to show her what she needed to learn from all of this and to replace her anger with His peace.

It wasn't an easy prayer to pray, but it was a necessary one. She realized that holding onto bitterness only multiplied her pain, while humility offered the possibility of true forgiveness and peace. Through this process, she understood that her peace couldn't be held hostage by their lack of remorse any longer. She needed to trust in God's work, both in their hearts and in hers.

This choice didn't erase the pain or the memories, but it did set her free from the chains of bitterness that had bound her for far too long. It was a small step towards healing, a step towards embracing forgiveness and finding peace within herself. And as she closed her eyes, she allowed a glimmer of hope to enter her heart—hope for a future unburdened by the weight of resentment, where forgiveness could flourish, and wounds could finally be mended.

Key Points

- Lysa chooses to send a birthday card to someone who had caused her deep hurt, as a gesture of forgiveness and healing.

- Frustrating news unrelated to the recipient of the card triggers intense anger and resentment within Lysa, as past hurts intertwine with the present situation.

- Lysa's counselor prompts her to reflect on her anger and question if it stems from a desire to see evidence of God defending her and bringing justice to those who hurt her.

- Lysa confronts her bitterness and chooses humility and surrender, offering her pain and resentment to God, releasing the need for revenge and justice.

- Through this process, Lysa learns to trust in God's work and finds freedom from the chains of bitterness, taking a step towards healing, forgiveness, and finding inner peace.

Milestone Goals

- Have you ever experienced a situation where you felt compelled to extend forgiveness to someone who had hurt you deeply? How did you navigate that process?

_____

_____

_____

- How do you understand the concept of bitterness and its effects on our emotions and perspectives?

_____

_____

_____

- Can you relate to the idea that our reactions to present situations can be influenced by unresolved past hurts? How have you seen this play out in your own life?

_____

_____

_____

- How do you personally approach the challenge of surrendering control and finding peace in situations where justice or apologies are not forthcoming?

_____

_____

_____

Action Plan

- Our past hurts can come back in the present and would be released on people that do not deserve it, if not controlled. Understand the need to address these issues.

_____

_____

_____

- Try to control your feelings of anger towards God. Whenever you feel like He has not been defending you, think of his unconditional love for you.

_____

_____

_____

- Release your need for justice and submit your pain into God's hands. Let your bitterness be taken away.

_____

_____

_____

Chapter 14 – Living the Practice of Forgiveness Everyday

Lysa sat at her desk, staring at the screen in disbelief. She had reached the last chapter of the book she had been reading, a book that had taken her on a journey of healing and self-discovery. Through its pages, she had faced her deepest hurts and learned the power of forgiveness. The progress she had made filled her with satisfaction, but also with a sense of fear. She was grateful for her healing, but she worried about living out this message of forgiveness in her future.

She couldn't ignore the impact that past wounds had on her heart. When hurt, she felt afraid and vulnerable, preferring to protect herself and hide rather than confront her resentments. She admitted that she was prone to holding grudges, drawn to the bitter rewards they seemed to offer. She realized that she couldn't unknow the teachings on forgiveness or ignore the dangers of bitterness creeping back into her heart.

Reflecting on the story of Adam and Eve, she saw her own tendency to hide when hurt. Fear and vulnerability led her to retreat, avoiding the harder conversations about boundaries and refusing to address her own issues. She knew that forgiving others wasn't easy, especially when they continued to hurt her. The temptation to dig up past wrongs and let bitterness consume her was strong.

Yet, amidst her wrestling with these feelings, she reached a realization: the goal of forgiveness wasn't perfection, but progress. She understood that occasional hesitation and resistance didn't make her a failure at forgiveness. She embraced her humanity, acknowledging that as a tenderhearted human, she was prone to deep feelings and vulnerability. She found solace in the Lord's Prayer, where Jesus emphasized the importance of confession and forgiveness. She recognized that forgiveness wasn't meant for only major heartbreaks but was a daily practice. She felt compelled to incorporate confession and forgiveness into her daily life, but she admitted that she hadn't been consistent in doing so.

Feeling a heavy burden within her, she realized that her reluctance to forgive and her struggles in relationships stemmed from her own emotional patterns. Conflict, chaos, and offense seemed to surround her, making her skeptical and defensive. She desired a change, a maturity that would enable her to approach relationships with empathy, patience, and trust. Determined to make progress, she developed a practical method using the Word of God as her guide. She chose verses from the Bible that addressed specific themes related to her relationship dynamics. Creating a journal, she drew a square and wrote the verse at the center, with the theme at the top and its opposite at the bottom. She divided the left side of the square, writing what God wanted her to do on the top and the enemy's response at the bottom.

The right side of the square held five words: progress, suppress, digress, regress, and confess. She used these prompts to evaluate her journey. She noted where she was making progress, where she encountered resistance, where she regressed, and where she rebelled against the verse. The process led her to confession and forgiveness, freeing her from the weight of unforgiveness and fostering personal growth. She understood that this continuous cycle of confession, forgiveness, and progress transformed her. It cultivated self-awareness, healthier perspectives, and deeper empathy. It strengthened her relationships and freed her from the cycle of offense and resentment. She realized that maturity wasn't the absence of hardships but the ability to let them work for her, adding to her development as a person.

One particular memory stood out in her mind, forever changing her view of forgiveness. A couple of years ago, during a visit to Israel, she had a transformative experience where women who lost their loved ones to war and politics came together for a peace talk. They all found forgiveness in each other's tears and sorrow.

As she closed the book, she felt a renewed sense of purpose. The journey toward forgiveness would be challenging, but she was determined to continue walking it. Each step would be an opportunity for growth, and she was ready to embrace it, knowing that progress, not perfection, was the goal. With hope in her heart, she closed her eyes, ready to embark on a new chapter of her life.

Key Points

- Lysa completed a book that has guided her on a journey of healing and self-discovery, particularly in the area of forgiveness.

- She acknowledges her tendency to hide and hold grudges when hurt but realizes that forgiveness is a daily practice and progress is more important than perfection.

- Lysa develops a practical method using the Word of God to guide her in relationships, incorporating confession, forgiveness, and progress.

- She recognizes the impact of emotional patterns on her reluctance to forgive and desires a change in maturity, empathy, patience, and trust.

- Lysa is inspired by a transformative experience in Israel, where women found forgiveness in each other's sorrow, and she embraces the journey toward forgiveness with renewed purpose and hope.

Milestone Goals

- Have you ever experienced the struggle of forgiveness in your own life? How did you navigate through it?

_____
_____
_____

- What steps or practices have you found helpful in cultivating forgiveness and letting go of grudges?

_____
_____
_____

- How do you balance the concept of progress in forgiveness with the natural human inclination to hold onto past hurts?

_____

_____

_____

- Can you share an example of a specific verse or passage from the Bible that has been particularly impactful in guiding you toward forgiveness?

_____

_____

_____

Action Plan

- Understand that the goal of forgiveness is not perfection but progress.

_____

_____

_____

- Once you figure out your emotional patterns, you will be able to forgive and let go of the resentment.

_____

_____

_____

- Pick a bible verse and analyze your progress, suppress, digress, regress, confess, and forgive consecutively.

_____

_____

_____

- Understand what compassion and forgiveness can accomplish in the human race and live up to the expectations of the Lord

_____
_____
_____

Lysa's Most Asked Questions

1. Sometimes the hardest part of forgiveness is forgiving myself. How do I do this?

Lysa reflected on the concept of forgiving oneself and the struggle she faced with feelings of shame and regret. She came to understand that forgiveness begins with God and cannot be self-generated. The enemy of your soul attempts to keep you trapped in condemnation and shame, hindering you from sharing the redemptive work of Jesus. Lysa shared her personal experience of carrying the weight of guilt and grief after making the decision to have an abortion. She longed for forgiveness but feels incapable of granting it to herself. Eventually, she discovered three key steps for you to receive God's forgiveness and release yourself from the burden of shame.

First, read Psalm 32:5, which prompts you to acknowledge your sin, confess it, and seek God's forgiveness openly. Realize the importance of having a witness to your confession, someone who can remind you of God's forgiveness. Second, verbalize your acceptance of God's forgiveness, reinforcing your memory of receiving His mercy. Understand that repentance accompanies faith and strive for a genuine expression of both. Finally, recognize that shame and accusation stem from the enemy, who seeks to keep your actions hidden and your heart burdened. Overcome your fear and resolve to share your story, allowing God to use your painful experience for good and find glimpses of redemption along the way.

Lysa's journey teaches you the power of compassion and the destructive nature of shame. Become tender-hearted, understanding the pain of making mistakes, and showing empathy towards others. Distinguish between compassion and excusing harmful behavior while striving to prevent others from carrying the weight of shame you once bore. Remember that shame and condemnation do not originate from God. Instead, confess, seek God's forgiveness, receive His grace, and live as a living testimony of redemption.

2. Forgiveness often is a regular part of relationships. But how do I know when my relationship has gotten to the place where it's unhealthy? In the chapter on boundaries, you talked about enabling. I've also heard the term codependency. What are the characteristics of codependency, and how does that show up in unhealthy relationships?

When you find yourself enabling the dysfunctional behavior of loved ones, it's essential to establish boundaries. The danger lies in rationalizing their actions, hoping that one day they will change and see you as their hero. However, this often leads to enabling their dysfunction. Terms like codependency and relationship addiction come into play when we prioritize others' needs above our own, sacrificing ourselves in the process. While the label of codependency may initially seem extreme, it can provide valuable awareness. Codependency involves being in a one-sided, dysfunctional relationship where someone relies on another for emotional and self-esteem needs, enabling their irresponsible behavior. It can occur in various types of relationships. Striving for balance through healthy assertiveness, rather than swinging between passivity and selfishness, is key to overcoming codependency. Recognizing these patterns empowers you to navigate relationships more effectively and prioritize your well-being.

Background Information About *Forgiving What You Can't Forget*

"Forgiving What You Can't Forget" is a compelling and transformative book written by Lysa TerKeurst. Drawing from her personal experiences of heartache and betrayal, TerKeurst delves into the complex and challenging topic of forgiveness. The book provides readers with practical guidance, biblical principles, and heartfelt insights on how to navigate the difficult process of forgiving those who have deeply hurt us.

TerKeurst's own journey of grappling with forgiveness and the pain of betrayal gives her a unique perspective and deep empathy for readers who are facing similar struggles. She shares her vulnerability and offers a safe space for readers to explore their own wounds and find healing.

With compassion and wisdom, TerKeurst explores the effects of unforgiveness on our emotional, mental, and spiritual well-being. She guides readers through the steps of forgiveness, highlighting the power of surrender, grace, and letting go of resentment.

"Forgiving What You Can't Forget" not only provides practical tools and strategies for forgiveness but also offers hope and encouragement for those who are burdened by past hurts. TerKeurst's engaging storytelling, relatable examples, and faith-filled approach make this book a valuable resource for anyone seeking to find freedom from the weight of unforgiveness and embrace a life of peace and restoration.

Background Information About Lysa TerKeurst

Lysa TerKeurst is a renowned author, speaker, and influential figure in the field of Christian living and women's empowerment. With her relatable and authentic approach, she has inspired millions of readers and listeners around the world.

Known for her vulnerability and transparency, she draws from her personal experiences to address topics such as forgiveness, healing, resilience, and faith. She has a unique ability to connect with her audience, offering practical insights and biblical wisdom to navigate life's challenges.

She is the founder of Proverbs 31 Ministries, a non-profit organization dedicated to encouraging and equipping women in their faith journeys. Through her ministry, she has created various resources, including books, devotionals, and online studies, all designed to empower women to live out their faith and pursue their God-given purpose.

Her bestselling books, such as "The Best Yes," "It's Not Supposed to Be This Way," and "Forgiving What You Can't Forget," have resonated with readers worldwide, providing them with guidance, encouragement, and inspiration to overcome adversity and grow spiritually.

Her relatability, authenticity, and deep faith have made her a sought-after speaker at conferences and events. Her powerful messages and engaging storytelling captivate audiences, leaving a lasting impact and inspiring individuals to live with renewed hope and purpose.

Overall, Lysa's work and ministry have touched countless lives, offering a compassionate and empowering voice to those seeking guidance, healing, and a deeper connection with God. Her words continue to uplift and encourage individuals to embrace their true identity, navigate life's challenges, and find joy in the journey of faith.

Trivia Questions

1.   What personal experiences does the author draw upon in the book?

2.   What are the 3 steps in delving into your past traumas and rising above them?

3.   What are some of the practical guidance and tools provided in the book for forgiveness?

4.   How does the author describe the effects of unforgiveness on our well-being?

5.   Can you recall a specific biblical principle mentioned in the book regarding forgiveness?

6.   How is loss attributed to the journey of forgiveness?

7.   How does the book explore the concept of letting go of bitterness?

8.   What overall message of hope and encouragement does the book offer to readers struggling with forgiveness?

9.   According to the book, why is forgiveness essential for our emotional, mental, and spiritual well-being?

10.   What is one of the main motivations TerKeurst offers for choosing to forgive those who have hurt us?

Discussion Questions

1. How does Lysa TerKeurst define forgiveness in "Forgiving What You Can't Forget," and how does her definition align with or differ from your own understanding of forgiveness?

2. In the book, TerKeurst emphasizes the importance of self-forgiveness. Discuss why self-forgiveness is crucial in the process of healing and moving forward.

3. TerKeurst talks about the concept of vulnerability in forgiveness. Have you faced a situation where being vulnerable has helped you in forgiving someone?

4. Forgiveness often involves confronting painful emotions and memories. How does TerKeurst guide readers in navigating and processing these emotions effectively?

5. TerKeurst suggests that forgiveness is a journey rather than a one-time event. Share your thoughts on this perspective and discuss practical ways to sustain forgiveness in the face of ongoing pain or triggers.

6. In the book, TerKeurst explores the relationship between forgiveness and trust. How does she address rebuilding trust after forgiveness has taken place? What insights or strategies does she offer?

7.   Forgiving someone who has deeply hurt us can be challenging. Discuss the role of empathy and compassion in the forgiveness process, as described by TerKeurst. How can cultivating empathy aid in our ability to forgive?

More books from Smart Reads

Summary of Breath: The New Science of a Lost Art By
    James Nestor
Workbook for What Happened to You? By Oprah Winfrey
    and Dr. Bruce Perry
Workbook for Limitless By Jim Kwik
Workbook for The Body Keeps the Score By Dr. Bessel van
    der Kolk
Workbook for Atlas of the Heart By Brené Brown
Workbook for Fast Like a Girl By Dr. Mindy Pelz
Workbook for The Tools By Phil Stutz and Barry Michels
Workbook for Glucose Revolution By Jessie Inchauspe

Thank You

Hope you've enjoyed your reading experience.

We here at Smart Reads will always strive to deliver to you the highest quality guides.

So I'd like to thank you for supporting us and reading until the very end.

Before you go, would you mind leaving us a review on Amazon?

It will mean a lot to us and support us creating high quality guides for you in the future.

Thanks once again!

Warmly yours,

The Smart Reads Team

Download Your Free Gift

As a way to say "Thank You" for being a fan of our series,
I've included a free gift for you:

Brain Health: How to Nurture and Nourish Your Brain For
Top Performance

Go to www.smart-reads.com to get your
FREE book.

The Smart Reads Team

Made in the USA
Las Vegas, NV
15 October 2023

79155119R00059